MEL BAY

EASIEST GUITAR THEORY BOOK

By Rob Goldsmith

1 2 3 4 5 6 7 8 9 0

Contents

Introduction 3

The "Building Blocks" 3

Scales 6

Chords 13

Inversions 19

Arpeggios 21

Larger Chords 23

Intervals 28

Chord Progressions 33

Rob Goldsmith is an active lounge and showroom guitarist in Las Vegas and holds Bachelor and Master of Music degrees from Southern Illinois University at Edwardsville.

Introduction

If you have been playing the guitar for a while, you've probably started to think about chords and scales, and wonder where they come from and how they are put together. This subject is known as **music theory.**

Popular music can range from a very simple and basic form to a type where much of it is very complex and uses ideas from many different styles of music. Understanding music theory can help a guitarist both in playing other people's songs and in creating original music.

Most music theory books are written using standard music notation. In this book, however, beginning music theory is taught using the guitar, and music reading is not needed. All of the information is shown on the guitar so that you can learn it and use it as quickly as possible. This book is designed so that you can either study it on your own or use it with a teacher. As you read it, play all of the examples on the guitar, so that you can hear what you are studying.

The "Building Blocks"

The basic "building blocks" of music theory are the half step, the whole step, and the musical alphabet. The half step is the smallest distance that can exist between any two notes. On the guitar, a half step is the distance from a note on one fret to a note on the next (higher or lower).

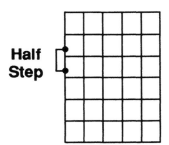

A whole step is equal to two half steps. On the guitar, that would be two frets.

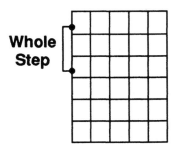

The musical alphabet is made up of the seven letters that are used to name the notes:

A B C D E F G

Each of the six strings of the guitar has a letter name:

E A D G B E

This letter name is for the note that you hear when the string is played open (no fingers on it). The musical alphabet can be played across the strings:

A D G

Or up a string:

A

4

Most of the notes in the musical alphabet have two frets between them (whole step). In two cases, B to C and E to F, there is only one fret from one note to the next (half step).

The notes "in between" the whole steps also have names. Their names have two parts:

    1) a musical alphabet letter
    2) the word "sharp" or "flat" after the letter

Sharp, which is abbreviated in music by ♯, means one half step higher. So, C sharp (C♯) is one half step (one fret) higher than C.

Fret   **A**
```
1
2
3     C
④     C♯
5
```

Flat, which is abbreviated in music by ♭, means one half step lower. So, D flat (D♭) would be one half step (one fret) lower than D.

Fret   **A**
```
1
2
3
④     D♭
5     D
```

Both of these notes are on the same fret. This shows a concept called **enharmonic,** where two notes that sound the same can have different names (C♯ = D♭).

Scales

If all of the whole steps in the musical alphabet are "filled in," it looks like this:

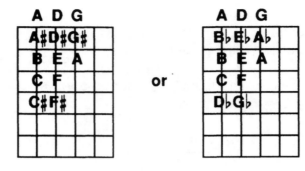

This arrangement of notes is called a **chromatic scale.** A **scale** is a group of notes that follows a certain arrangement of whole and half steps. A chromatic scale is a scale of half steps. When it is played **ascending** (from low to high notes), sharps are used to name the notes:

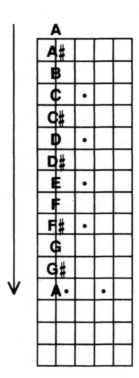

When it is played **descending** (from high to low notes), flats are used to name the notes:

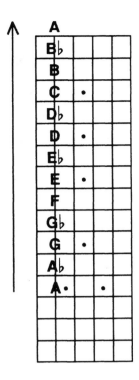

Most scales are written for one **octave.** An octave is the distance from one note to the next note with the same name (higher or lower).

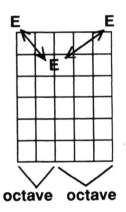

Here are the notes in a one-octave descending chromatic scale (from A to A):

A	A♭	G	G♭	F	E	E♭	D	D♭	C	B	B♭	A
1	2	3	4	5	6	7	8	9	10	11	12	1

There are twelve different notes, then the first repeats, but it is one octave lower than the first note of the scale. If the scale were to continue for another octave, it would repeat the same twelve notes one octave lower. All of the other scales that will be studied in this book will use some combination of these twelve notes, or their **enharmonic equivalents** (the sharp versions — that is, G♯ instead of A♭, F♯ instead of G♭, etc.).

This chart shows sharped notes and their flatted equivalents:

A♯	B♯	C♯	D♯	E♯	F♯	G♯
B♭	C	D♭	E♭	F	G♭	A♭

Compare the diagrams for the two chromatic scales and see how the sharped and flatted notes match up.

The basic scale, from which all others will be formed is the **major scale.** All scales are named by their type and by their starting note. Here are the notes in a C major scale:

C	D	E	F	G	A	B	C
1	2	3	4	5	6	7	1

It can be played across the strings, like this:

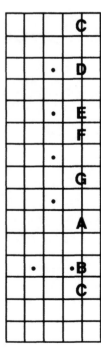

If it is played on one string, it looks like this:

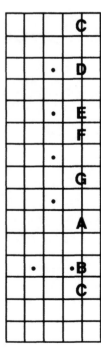

Looking at the scale on one string, it's easy to figure out the distance between each note:

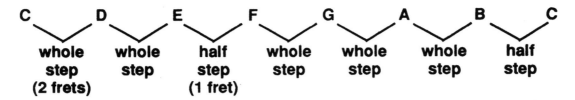

This order of whole and half steps can become a formula for major scales. Starting on any of the notes of the chromatic scale, if this order of whole and half steps is followed, a major scale is built.

For example — start on G:

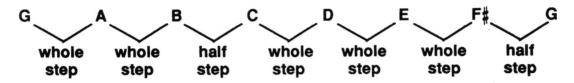

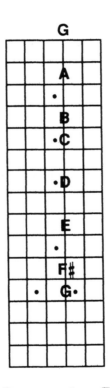

Or — start on F:

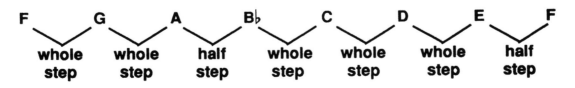

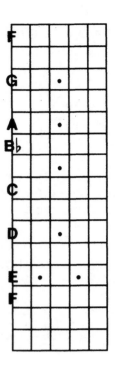

In addition to the "formula," the basic order of the musical alphabet is followed, so that no letter name is used twice in a row. This is the reason why the fourth note in the F major scale is B♭ instead of being called A♯.

Here are major scales starting on the twelve notes of the chromatic scale. Try playing each of these up one string, like the previous examples:

1	2	3	4	5	6	7
C	D	E	F	G	A	B
D♭	E♭	F	G♭	A♭	B♭	C
D	E	F♯	G	A	B	C♯
E♭	F	G	A♭	B♭	C	D
E	F♯	G♯	A	B	C♯	D♯
F	G	A	B♭	C	D	E
G♭	A♭	B♭	C♭	D♭	E♭	F
G	A	B	C	D	E	F♯
A♭	B♭	C	D♭	E♭	F	G
A	B	C♯	D	E	F♯	G♯
B♭	C	D	E♭	F	G	A
B	C♯	D♯	E	F♯	G♯	A♯

Here is a popular fingering for a two-octave major scale. This uses no open strings and can be moved up and down the neck in order to play the scale in different **keys,** or from different starting notes.

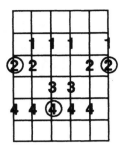

The numbers are finger numbers, and the circled numbers show where the starting note or **tonic** of the scale is.

Other scales can be built by changing some notes in the major scale. To show this, the numbers that represent the notes of the major scale will be used:

1   2   3   4   5   6   7

As an example, here is a scale whose fingering will probably look very familiar:

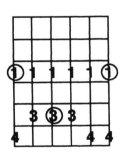

This is the minor pentatonic scale, which is one of the most common scales used in rock soloing. Its formula would be:

1   ♭3   4   5   ♭7

This means that, in comparison to a major scale, the minor pentatonic scale uses the first, fourth and fifth notes, along with the **flatted** third and seventh notes.

For example:

C major	=	C	D	E	F	G	A	B
C minor pentatonic	=	C		E♭	F	G		B♭
A major	=	A	B	C♯	D	E	F♯	G♯
A minor pentatonic	=	A		C	D	E		G

11

Some other important scales are:

Harmonic minor: 1   2   ♭3   4   5   ♭6   7

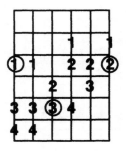

Natural minor: 1   2   ♭3   4   5   ♭6   ♭7

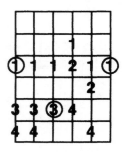

Melodic minor (ascending):   1   2   ♭3   4   5   6   7

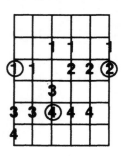

Melodic minor (descending):   Same as natural minor

Note: The melodic minor scale is the only scale that uses a different formula descending and ascending.

Dorian: 1   2   ♭3   4   5   6   ♭7

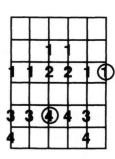

To really learn these scales, each one should be **written** out using all twelve starting notes, **played** on the guitar, and **sung,** using either actual note names or scale numbers, in order to really hear the sound of the scale.

Chords

Scales are the basic tools for melody in music. **Chords** (groups of three or more notes, played at the same time) can be built from the notes in a scale. Chords are the basic tools for **harmony** in music. The most basic chords are three-note chords, known as **triads.**

There are four types of triads:

1) Major
2) Minor
3) Augmented
4) Diminished

A major triad is built from the first, third and fifth steps of a major scale. For example, here is a C major scale:

C	D	E	F	G	A	B
1	2	3	4	5	6	7

The notes for a C major chord would be:

C	D	E	F	G	A	B
1		3		5		

Here is one way to play a C major chord:

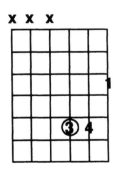 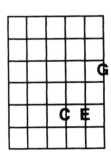

The chord's letter name, which comes from the first step of the scale, is known as the **root** of the chord.

So, just as major scales can be built from any note, so can major chords, using this formula: 1–3–5.

For example:

F major scale = F   G   A   B♭   C   D   E
F major chord = F – A – C   (1–3–5 from scale)

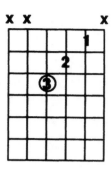
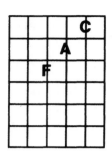

A major scale = A   B   C♯   D   E   F♯   G♯
A major chord = A – C♯ – E   (1–3–5 from scale)

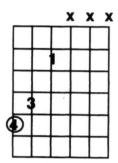
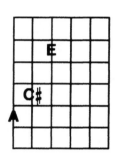

When talking about major scales and chords, often the word "major" is left out. So, if someone talks about an F chord or a G scale, for example, assume F **major** chord or G **major** scale.

Here are major triads built on all twelve notes of the chromatic scale:

1	3	5
C	E	G
B	D♯	F♯
B♭	D	F
A	C♯	E
A♭	C	E♭
G	B	D

1	3	5
G♭	B♭	D♭
F	A	C
E	G♯	B
E♭	G	B♭
D	F♯	A
D♭	F	A♭

Play each one using the fingerings in the previous examples. No open strings are used in these fingerings, so they can be moved up and down the neck to get different chords. For example, if the C chord is moved down two frets, it would be a B♭ chord.

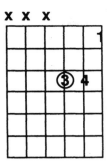 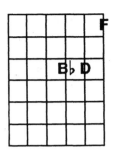

Or, if the F chord is moved up one fret, it becomes a G♭ chord.

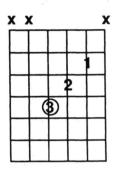 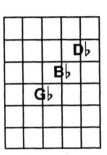

Memorizing the spelling of all twelve major triads, as shown in the chart, can be really helpful for future studying.

As mentioned earlier, the note of the chord that comes from the first step of the scale is also known as the **root** of the chord. The chord tone that comes from the third step of the scale is known as the **third,** and similarly the chord tone that comes from the fifth step of the scale is called the **fifth.**

The formula for a major triad can be changed to give formulas for the other three types of triads. If the third of a major triad is lowered one half step, a minor triad is formed.

Major = 1–3–5
Minor = 1–♭3–5

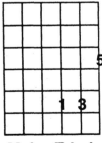 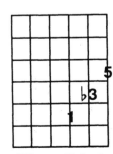

Major Triad   **Minor Triad**

15

If the fifth of a major triad is raised one half step, an augmented triad is formed.

Major = 1–3–5
Augmented = 1–3–♯5

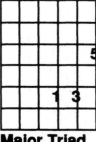 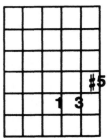

Major Triad   **Augmented Triad**

If the third and fifth of a major triad are each lowered one half step, a diminished triad is formed.

Major = 1–3–5
Diminished = 1–♭3–♭5

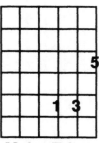 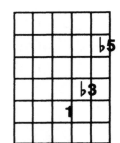

Major Triad   **Diminished Triad**

Here are all four triads, built on C:

C major = C–E–G
C minor = C–E♭–G (lowered third one half step)
C augmented = C–E–G♯ (raised fifth one half step)
C diminished = C–E♭–G♭ (lowered third and fifth one half step)

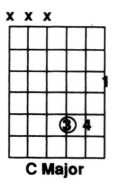 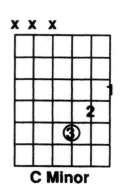 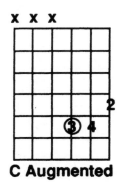 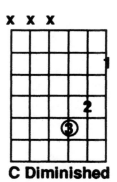

C Major   **C Minor**   **C Augmented**   **C Diminished**

In order to change all the chords, two new symbols are needed:

1) To flat a note that is already flatted, use a double flat (𝄫).

Example: B♭ lowered one half step = B𝄫

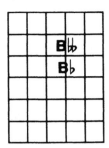

2) To sharp a note that is already sharped, use a double sharp (𝄪).

Example: F♯ raised one half step = F𝄪

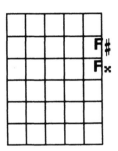

These double sharped and double flatted notes actually could be called by other names. For example, B𝄫 is the same note as A, and F𝄪 is the same note as G.

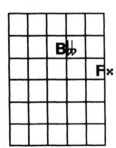
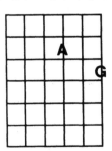

The reason that the double sharp and double flat notes are used is that, when triads are written, they can't use two letters of the musical alphabet that are right next to each other. So, for example, that's why a G♭ minor triad has to be written G♭–B𝄫–D♭. If it were written G♭–A–D♭, two of the notes (G and A) would be breaking the "alphabet rule," since they are next to each other in the musical alphabet.

All four triads in B:

B major = B–D♯–F♯
B minor = B–D–F♯
B augmented = B–D♯–F×
B diminished = B–D–F

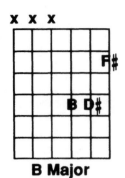

B Major

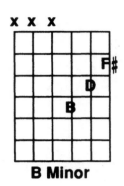

B Minor

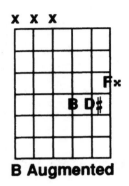

B Augmented

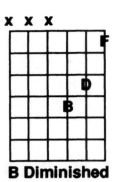

B Diminished

All four triads in G♭:

G♭ major = G♭–B♭–D♭
G♭ minor = G♭–B♭♭–D♭
G♭ augmented = G♭–B♭–D
G♭ diminished = G♭–B♭♭–D♭♭

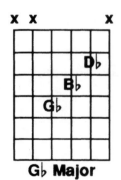

G♭ Major

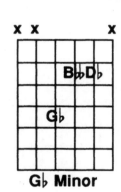

G♭ Minor

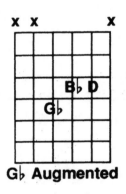

G♭ Augmented

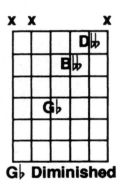

G♭ Diminished

You should write out all four triads using each note of the chromatic scale as the root. Use both the sharped and the flatted notes. For example, even though C♯ and D♭ sound the same, the triads built from these notes are spelled very differently.

C♯ major = C♯–E♯–G♯	D♭ major = D♭–F–A♭
C♯ minor = C♯–E–G♯	D♭ minor = D♭–F♭–A♭
C♯ augmented = C♯–E♯–G×	D♭ augmented = D♭–F–A
C♯ diminished = C♯–E–G	D♭ diminished = D♭–F♭–A♭♭

Instead of using just three strings, most guitar chords use four, five or six strings, like these:

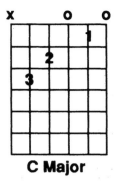

C Major

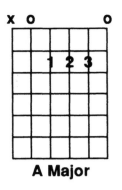

A Major

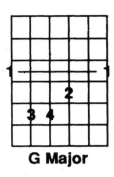

G Major

In these forms, even though more strings are being used, only three different notes (letter names) are in each chord:

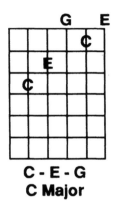

C - E - G
C Major

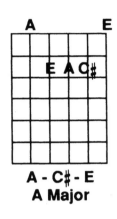

A - C♯ - E
A Major

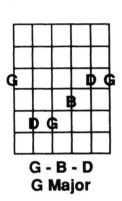

G - B - D
G Major

This concept is called **doubling.** Repeating certain notes of a chord (especially the root and fifth) makes the chord sound "bigger." These chords are still considered triads, since there are still just **three different** notes in each chord.

Inversions

So far, the triads shown have all had the root as the lowest (or bottom) note of the chord. Chords can also be written with other tones as the lowest; these are called **inversions.**

When the root of a chord is on the bottom, this is called **root position.** When the third of a chord is on the bottom, this is called **first inversion.**

Example:

C major (root position) = C–E–G
C major (first inversion) = E–G–C or E–C–G

19

Notice that both forms have the same three notes, just in a different order. Here is one way that these can be played:

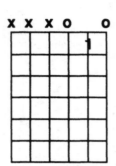

C Major: Root Position

C Major: First Inverstion

When the fifth of a chord is on the bottom, this is called **second inversion.**

C major (second inversion) = G–C–E or G–E–C

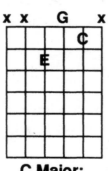

C Major: Second Inversion

Chords can also be arranged in either close or open voicing. In close voicing, the notes are as close together as possible, creating a very "tight" sound.

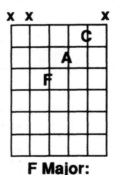

**C Major:
Close Voicing**

**F Major:
Close Voicing**

In open voicing, the middle note of a triad is moved an octave from its close voicing position, to create a more "spacious" sound.

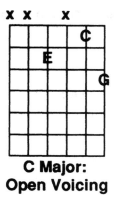

C Major:
Open Voicing

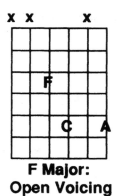

F Major:
Open Voicing

Arpeggios

When the notes of a chord are played one by one, rather than strummed all at once, this is known as an **arpeggio.** Arpeggios are usually played one of three ways:

1) Holding down a chord form with the left hand and picking the strings individually.

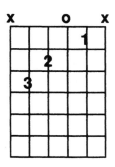

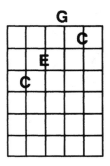

This shows a C major chord, where the notes played individually from lowest to highest make a one-octave C major arpeggio. (That is, the notes spell out a C major chord one time and end on the root one octave higher.)

2) Picking out the notes of the chord from a scale fingering pattern.

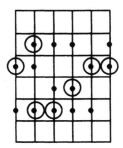

Above is a two-octave major scale. The circled notes are the notes that make up the major chord that comes from this scale. If these notes are played one at a time, from lowest to highest, this makes a **two-octave** major arpeggio. (The notes of the chord are played twice.)

If the "extra" scale notes are taken out, the arpeggio fingering is easier to see and remember.

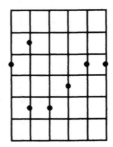

Here are two good fingerings for this pattern:

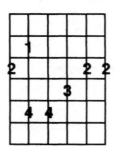 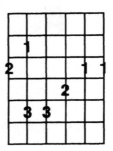

3) Using a fingering pattern with one note per string, so that a "sweep picking" technique can be used. Here are several fingerings for a major arpeggio that use this approach:

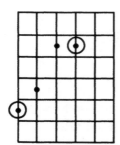 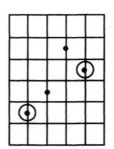 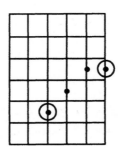

Every type of chord can be played as an arpeggio. Here are some arpeggio fingerings for the other three types of triads:

Minor Arpeggios

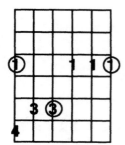 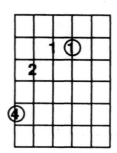 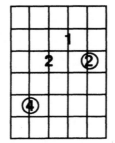 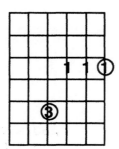

Augmented Arpeggios

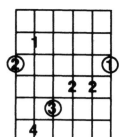 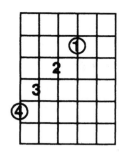 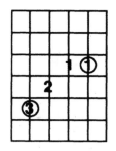 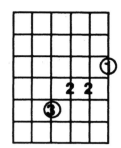

Diminished Arpeggios

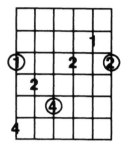 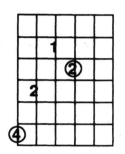 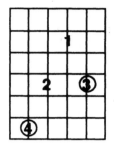 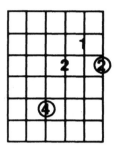

Larger Chords

In addition to triads, there are also chords that have four, five, or six different notes in them. Just like triads, they use a formula of notes taken from the major scale, but with these chords, a two-octave scale is used (two times through the notes).

C	D	E	F	G	A	B		C	D	E	F	G	A	B
		first octave								**second octave**				

The notes of the first octave are numbered as before:

C	D	E	F	G	A	B
1	2	3	4	5	6	7

Then, for the second octave, the numbers continue:

C	D	E	F	G	A	B		C	D	E	F	G	A	B
1	2	3	4	5	6	7		8	9	10	11	12	13	14
		first octave								**second octave**				

Here are some examples of these larger chords:

The major 6th chord adds the sixth note of the scale to the major triad. The formula is 1–3–5–6. In the key of C, the notes are C–E–G–A. Here are a chord fingering and an arpeggio fingering for a major 6th chord:

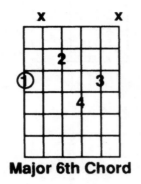
Major 6th Chord

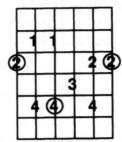
Major 6th Arpeggio

The major 7th chord adds the seventh note of the scale to the major triad. The formula is 1–3–5–7. In the key of C, the notes are C–E–G–B.

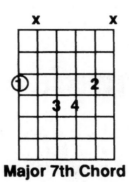
Major 7th Chord

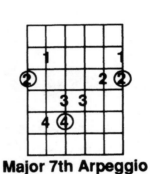
Major 7th Arpeggio

The minor 7th chord adds the **flatted** seventh note of the scale to the minor triad. The formula is 1–♭3–5–♭7. In the key of C, the notes are C–E♭–G–B♭.

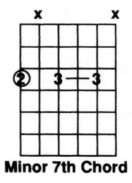
Minor 7th Chord

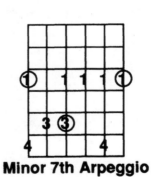
Minor 7th Arpeggio

The dominant 7th chord, also known as a 7th chord, adds the flatted seventh note of the scale to the major triad. The formula is 1–3–5–♭7. In the key of C, the notes are C–E–G–B♭.

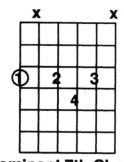
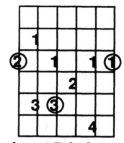

Dominant 7th Chord   **Dominant 7th Arpeggio**

Another family of larger chords is the ninth chords. They are five-note chords in theory, but when played on the guitar, one note is usually left out to make it easier to finger. For example, the major 9th chord adds the seventh and ninth notes of the scale to the major triad. The formula is 1–3–5–7–9. In the key of C, the notes are C–E–G–B–D. Here are the fingerings for a four-note version, which leaves out the fifth, and a five-note version, which contains all of the notes, but is harder to finger:

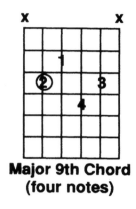
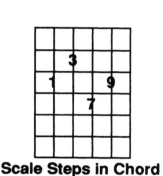

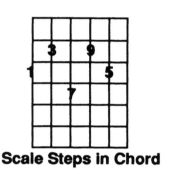

Major 9th Chord (four notes)   **Scale Steps in Chord**   **Major 9th Chord (five notes)**   **Scale Steps in Chord**

Since the arpeggio is played one note at a time, all of the notes can be played.

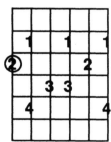

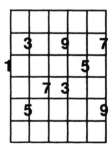

Major 9th Arpeggio   **Scales Steps in Arpeggio**

The minor 9th chord adds the flatted seventh and the natural (not altered) ninth to the minor triad. The formula is 1–♭3–5–♭7–9. In the key of C, the notes are C–E♭–G–B♭–D. There is a fingering for this chord that uses all five notes, as well as one that again leaves out the fifth. Play both of them and compare the sound. The fifth can be left out of larger chords like these without destroying the sound of the chord.

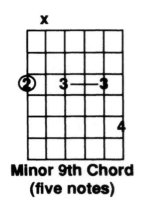

**Minor 9th Chord
(five notes)**

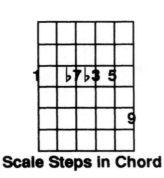

Scale Steps in Chord

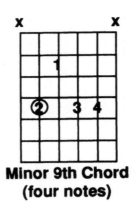

**Minor 9th Chord
(four notes)**

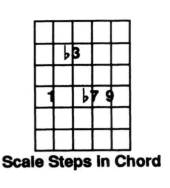

Scale Steps in Chord

The arpeggio, again, has all of the notes:

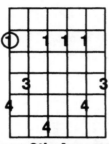

Minor 9th Arpeggio

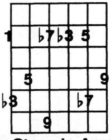

Scale Steps in Arpeggio

The dominant 9th chord, also known as a 9th chord, adds the flatted seventh and the natural ninth to the major triad. The formula is 1–3–5–♭7–9. In the key of C, the notes are C–E–G–B♭–D. Here are two chord fingerings, a four-note and a five-note, and an arpeggio:

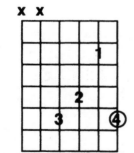

(Dominant) 9th Chord

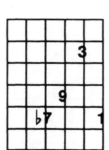

Scale Steps in Chord

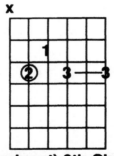

(Dominant) 9th Chord

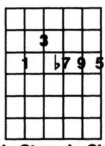

Scale Steps in Chord

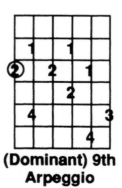

**(Dominant) 9th
Arpeggio**

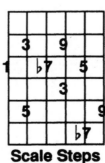

**Scale Steps
in Arpeggio**

There are many other types of chords that won't be mentioned in this book. However, they are all built from these chords, either by adding or changing certain notes. One special four-note chord is the diminished 7th chord. It is built by adding the **double flatted** seventh to the diminished triad. The formula is 1–♭3–♭5–♭♭7. In the key of C, the notes are C–E♭–G♭–B♭♭. The interesting thing about this chord is that any of the notes of the chord can be the root, and the chord remains the same.

For example:

Diminished 7th formula = 1–♭3–♭5–♭♭7
C diminished 7th = C–E♭–G♭–B♭♭ (B♭♭ = A)
E♭ diminished 7th = E♭–G♭–B♭♭–D♭♭ (D♭♭ = C)
G♭ diminished 7th = G♭–B♭♭–D♭♭–F♭♭ (F♭♭ = E♭)
A diminished 7th = A–C–E♭–G♭

The same four notes make up each of these four chords, so that each chord fingering could be called any one of the four chords.

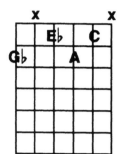 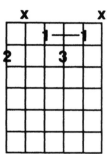 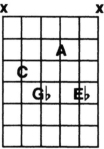

C Diminished 7th Chord
or E♭ Diminished 7th Chord
or G♭ Diminished 7th Chord
or A Diminished 7th Chord

C Diminished 7th Chord
or E♭ Diminished 7th Chord
or G♭ Diminished 7th Chord
or A Diminished 7th Chord

The arpeggio works the same way. Any of the four notes could act as the root (starting note).

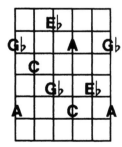

C Diminished 7th Arpeggio
or E♭ Diminished 7th Arpeggio
or G♭ Diminished 7th Arpeggio
or A Diminished 7th Arpeggio

Intervals

Another important part of music theory is **intervals.** An interval is the musical distance between any two notes. Let's start by looking at a major scale and its formula:

$$1 - 2 - 3 - 4 - 5 - 6 - 7 - 8$$
$$\text{W} \quad \text{W} \quad \text{H} \quad \text{W} \quad \text{W} \quad \text{W} \quad \text{H}$$

The distance between 1 and 2, a whole step, can also be called the interval of a **major second.** The distance between 1 and 3, two whole steps, is called the interval of a **major third.** Let's continue this idea:

scale steps	number of steps	interval
1 to 2	one whole step	major second
1 to 3	two whole steps	major third
1 to 4	two and one-half	perfect fourth
1 to 5	three and one-half	perfect fifth
1 to 6	four and one-half	major sixth
1 to 7	five and one-half	major seventh
1 to 8	six whole steps	perfect octave

So, in a C major scale (C–D–E–F–G–A–B–C), the intervals from the root (C) are:

C to D = major second
C to E = major third
C to F = perfect fourth
C to G = perfect fifth
C to A = major sixth
C to B = major seventh
C to C = perfect octave

Here is one way to play these intervals on the guitar:

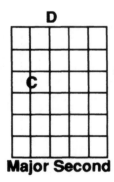

Major Second

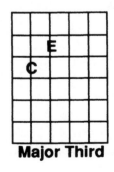

Major Third

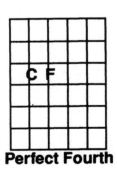

Perfect Fourth

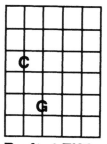
Perfect Fifth

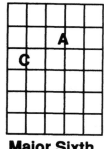
Major Sixth

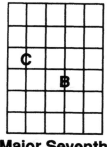
Major Seventh

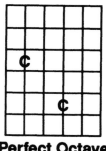
Perfect Octave

If both notes are played at the same time, this is called a **harmonic interval.** If the notes are played individually, then it is called a **melodic interval.**

Just like with chords, the formula for intervals can be used to build any interval from any scale. For example, take an F major scale:

F–G–A–B♭–C–D–E–F
F to G = major second
F to A = major third
F to B♭ = perfect fourth
F to C = perfect fifth
F to D = major sixth
F to E = major seventh
F to F = perfect octave

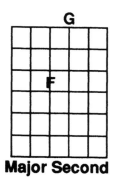
Major Second

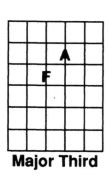
Major Third

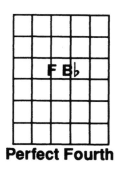
Perfect Fourth

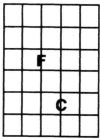
Perfect Fifth

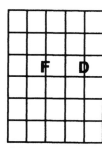
Major Sixth

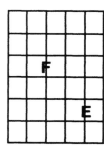
Major Seventh

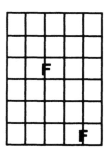
Perfect Octave

Intervals can also be used to describe the musical distance between the notes in a chord. Let's look at a C major triad (C–E–G).

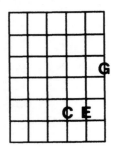

The distance from C to E is a major third, or two whole steps.

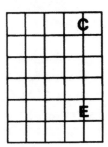

The distance from E to G is one and one-half steps. This is known as a **minor** third. Any major interval that is made smaller by a half step is known as a minor interval.

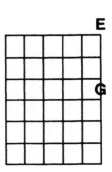

All four basic triads are made up of different combinations of major and minor third intervals. As shown above, the major triad is made up of a major third and a minor third:

C   –   E   –   G
    major   **minor**
    third   **third**

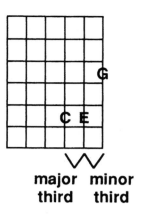

major   minor
third   third

The minor triad is made up of a minor third and a major third:

C   –   **E♭**   –   **G**

    minor   major
    third   third

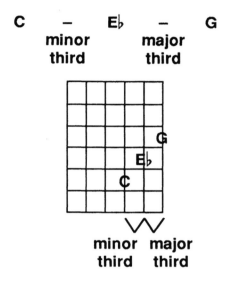

minor   major
third   third

The diminished triad is made up of two minor thirds:

C   –   **E♭**   –   **G♭**

    minor   minor
    third   third

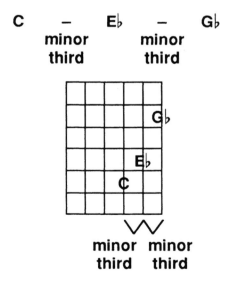

minor   minor
third   third

And, the augmented triad is made up of two major thirds:

C   –   E   –   G♯

   major   **major**
   third   **third**

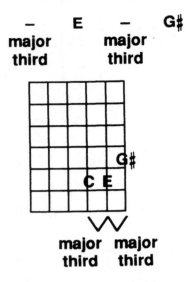

major   major
third   third

Most larger chords are also made up of major and minor thirds:

C major 7   =   **C**   –   **E**   –   **G**   –   **B**

      major   **minor**   **major**
      third   **third**   **third**

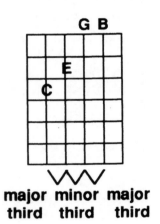

major   minor   major
third   third   third

A minor 7   =   **A**   –   **C**   –   **E**   –   **G**

      minor   **major**   **minor**
      third   **third**   **third**

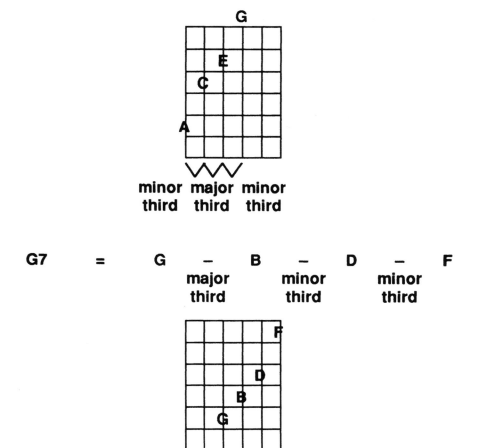

There are other intervals that can exist in chords, especially when using inversions, but they won't be studied in this book.

Chord Progressions

A study of chords leads to **chord progressions.** A chord progression is a certain order of chords that normally makes up a song. For example, a folk or country song could include this chord progression:

$$\text{G} \quad \text{C} \ | \ \text{G} \quad \text{D7} \ | \ \text{G} \quad \text{C} \ | \ \text{G} \quad \text{D7} \quad \text{G}$$
/ / / / | / / / / | / / / / | / / /

(Each diagonal line means to strum the chord once.)

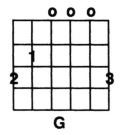
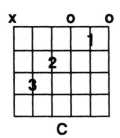
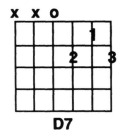

33

Play this chord progression several times, and hear how it sounds like it could be a song if it had a melody to go with the chords. Also notice that, after the last chord is played, the progression sounds finished. This introduces the concept of **key** or **key center.**

The key or key center of a chord progression is the note or chord on which the chord progression is based. Most chord progressions end on a chord built on the keynote, or first note of the key. Many chord progressions, like the example above, both end and start on a chord built on the keynote. This chord is known as the **tonic** chord of the key, because it is built on the first note of the key.

Many musicians use numbers instead of chord names when talking about chord progressions. Each chord is numbered from the scale built from the keynote. Let's take the same chord progression example and change the letter names to numbers.

This progression both ends and starts with a G major chord, and sounds finished after the last chord, so it is in the key of G major. That means that the chords in the progression come from the G major scale:

G	A	B	C	D	E	F#
1	2	3	4	5	6	7

Now, let's replace the chord letter names with the numbers that match up with the letters:

```
1  4  |  1  5  |  1  4  |  1  5  1
/ / / / | / / / / | / / / / | /   /   /
```

Using numbers makes it very easy to **transpose** this progression, which means to put it into another key. Let's say that you were singing a song using this chord progression in G major, but some of the notes were a little too high. You could transpose it down one step to the key of F major.

Take the F major scale and number the notes:

F	G	A	Bb	C	D	E
1	2	3	4	5	6	7

Then match the notes from this scale with the numbers in the progression:

```
1  4   |  1  5   |  1  4   |  1  5  1
F  Bb  |  F  C7  |  F  Bb  |  F  C7  F
/ / / / | / / / / | / / / / | /   /   /
```

34

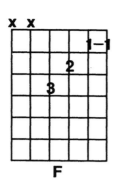

F

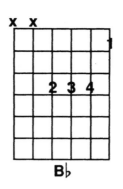

B♭

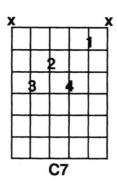

C7

Play this progression. Notice that it sounds similar to the first progression. The only difference is that all of the chords are from the key of F major, which is one step lower than the original progression.

Using this system, any chord progression or song can be transposed into another key. The number system also makes it easier to learn songs. For example, many songs are based on a 1–4–5 progression:

$$1 \quad | 4 \quad | 1 \quad | 1^7 \quad | 4 \quad | 4 \quad |$$
$$/ \ / \ / \ / \ | \ / \ / \ / \ / \ | \ / \ / \ / \ / \ | \ / \ / \ / \ / \ | \ / \ / \ / \ / \ | \ / \ / \ / \ / \ |$$

$$1 \quad | 1^7 \quad | 5^7 \quad | 4 \quad | 1 \quad | 1 \quad |$$
$$/ \ / \ / \ / \ | \ / \ / \ / \ / \ | \ / \ / \ / \ / \ | \ / \ / \ / \ / \ | \ / \ / \ / \ / \ | \ / \ / \ / \ / \ |$$

This progression can easily be put into any key using the scale number system. If you learn songs by numbers, and not just by chord names, you will see that many songs are based on the same chord progressions in different keys.

Let's put this progression into the key of E:

$$\begin{array}{ccccccccccccccc} \text{E major scale} & = & E & - & F\sharp & - & G\sharp & - & A & - & B & - & C\sharp & - & D\sharp \\ & & 1 & & 2 & & 3 & & 4 & & 5 & & 6 & & 7 \end{array}$$

$$1 = E \quad 4 = A \quad 5 = B$$

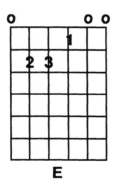

E

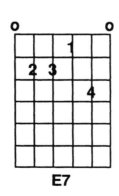

E7

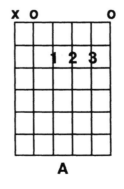

A

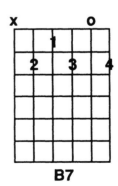

B7

Now, let's transpose this progression to the key of A major:

A major scale   =   A – B – C# – D – E – F# – G#
                    1   2   3   4   5   6   7

1 = A   4 = D   5 = E

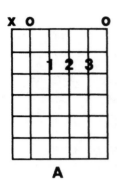
A

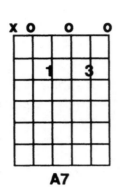
A7

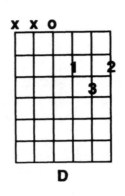
D

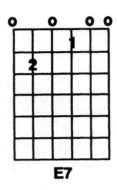
E7

Play both of these progressions, and again notice how they sound similar, even though you are playing different chords.

I hope that you have enjoyed and learned from this book. If you would like to learn more about music and music theory (and there is lots more to learn), there are many other good books and teachers available. Learning to read music would be a great help for learning more about the guitar and music in general. If you study and practice the information in this book, you will have a great foundation on which to continue building your musical knowledge.

Good luck and have lots of fun with music and the guitar!

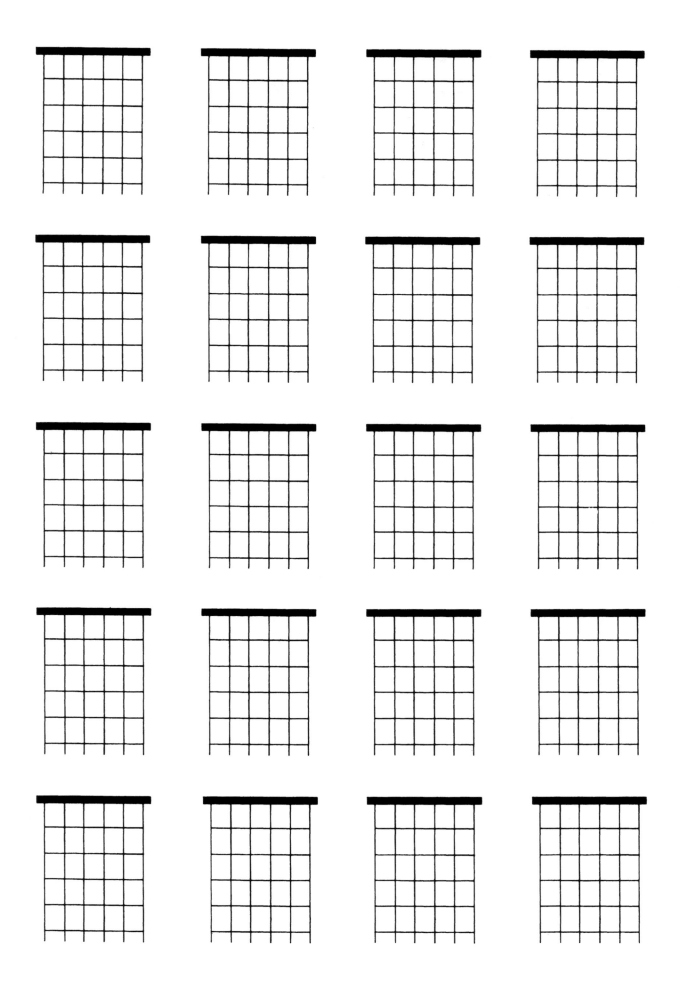

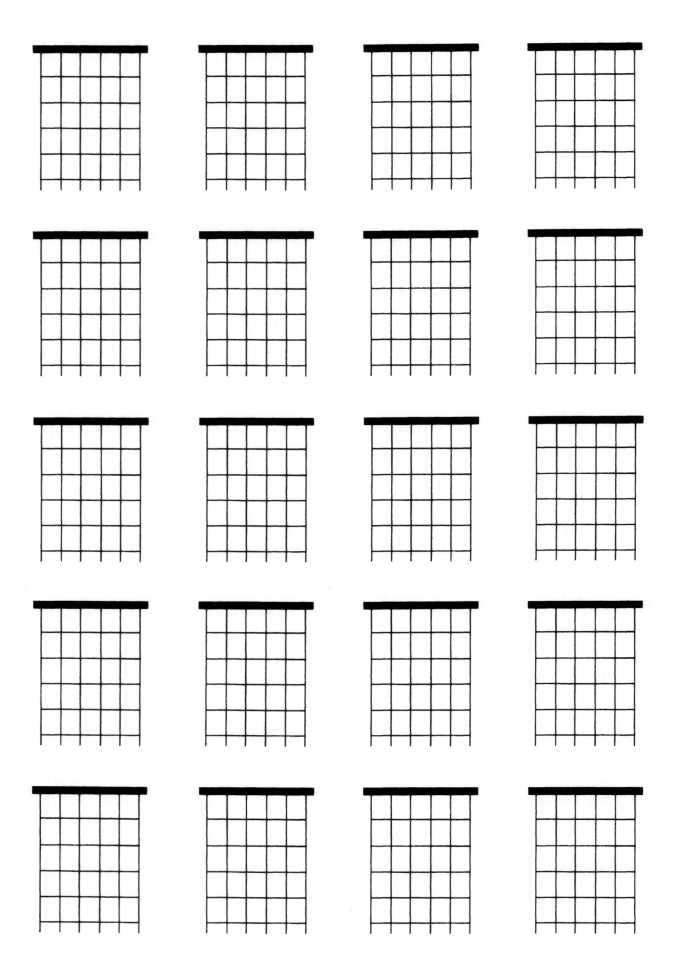

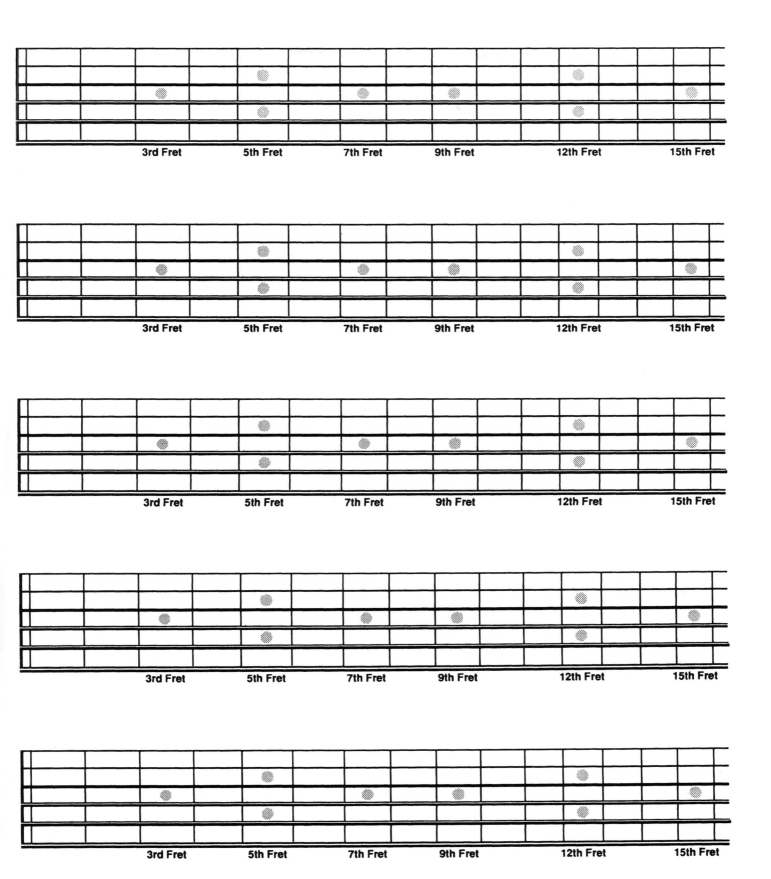

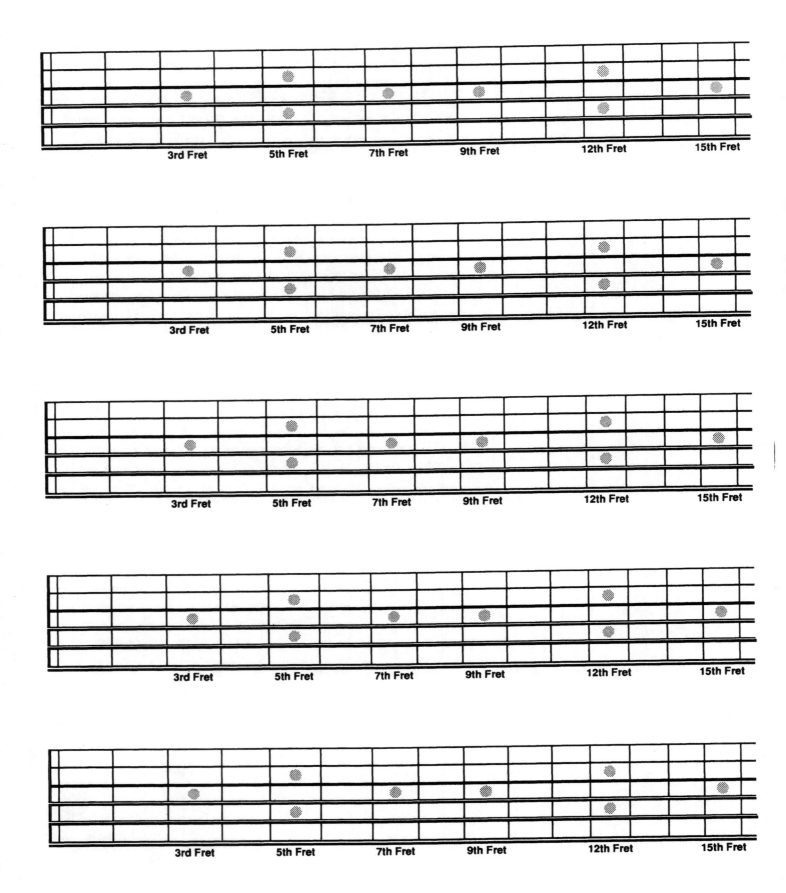

3rd Fret 5th Fret 7th Fret 9th Fret 12th Fret 15th Fret

3rd Fret 5th Fret 7th Fret 9th Fret 12th Fret 15th Fret

3rd Fret 5th Fret 7th Fret 9th Fret 12th Fret 15th Fret

3rd Fret 5th Fret 7th Fret 9th Fret 12th Fret 15th Fret

3rd Fret 5th Fret 7th Fret 9th Fret 12th Fret 15th Fret